For information address N&J Publishing 200 North End Avenue New York, New York 10282
Manufactured in China
First Edition, August 2021   10 9 8 7 6 5 4 3 2 1
ISBN: 978-1-7367886-8-4
For more information visit us at www.TheMagicalTales.com

MICKEY & FRIENDS

MICKEY'S Magical CHRISTMAS

This Book Belongs to

_____

_____

Illustrated by **the Disney Storybook Art Team**
Written by **Nathalie Martinez**
Designed by **Maureen Mulligan**

On Christmas Eve, Donald, Goofy, Daisy, and Minnie arrived in their winter's best to Mickey and Pluto's house. Mickey was so excited to share his new idea with his friends for the special party he had planned.

"Oh Mickey! I can't wait for the **Christmas** festivities!" Minnie said.

"Oh boy, do we have a fun day ahead!" Mickey exclaimed.

This year, Mickey and his friends were doing things a bit differently.

"Let's share our favorite **Christmas traditions** together!" Mickey said.

"Great idea, Mickey!" Minnie added. She put on her hat and continued, "Let's all put on our Santa hats to get in the Christmas spirit!"

They all thought that it was a fantastic idea, and could hardly wait to start celebrating!

◆ Tradition 1 ◆

Join Mickey and Friends and
let the celebrations begin by putting on your Santa hat!

Mickey's friends were excited, and ready for the Christmas fun to start.
Mickey shouted, **"Let the festivities ... begin!"**

"It isn't Christmas without **decorating** the tree!" Daisy said. "I just love adding the star to the top of the tree, it makes it feel **magical**."

✦ Tradition 2 ✦

Play your favorite Christmas music to get in the holiday spirit, as you adorn your tree with your favorite ornaments!

"Great idea, Daisy! Let's start with **tree trimming**!" Mickey said.

8

Goofy encouraged his friends to take part in this Christmas tradition. "Everyone, grab an **ornament** and make the tree look jolly!" Goofy said.

Daisy and Minnie hung the ornaments, while the rest of the friends made sure they had the tools they needed to decorate!

"I love seeing everyone in the **Christmas spirit**!" Mickey said.

"The place is starting to look really joyful!" Daisy said.

Once the friends were done with their first Christmas activity, they posed behind the tree while Donald took a picture!

"Doesn't it look great, Donald?" Daisy said.

Indeed it did!

✦ Tradition 3 ✦

Time for family portraits! Take a picture by your tree to create a lasting memory of your holiday together.

Before they picked their next activity, Pluto ran to grab stockings.
"Good boy, Pluto! Looks like he wants to share his favorite activity." Mickey said. Pluto
loved **stockings** because his favorite treat was usually in them, bones!

Daisy thought it'd be special to personalize each stocking with their name.
"Now they're ready to put up by the fireplace," Daisy said.

✦ Tradition 4 ✦

Personalize stockings for you and your family.
Hang them where Santa can add special surprises!

When they were done putting up stockings, they moved to the kitchen for a snack.

"Cheers to eating my favorite treats!" Donald said with a quack.

They all enjoyed their candy canes, and celebrated being together.
"This is the best **Christmas party**!" Minnie added.

◆ Tradition 5 ◆

Delight in your favorite holiday treat!
Bonus: Make it extra special by baking it together.

Now that their stomachs were full, and their hearts warm, Mickey figured it was the best time to share his tradition with his friends.

"I love writing **letters to Santa**!" Mickey said. "The trick is to ask for something you really want!"